THE CHALLENGE OF MERCY

THE CHALLENGE OF MERCY

Christian Life in Today's World

WALTER KASPER

Paulist Press
New York / Mahwah, NJ

Cover image by NatalyFox/Shutterstock.com
Cover and book design by Lynn Else

Library of Congress Cataloging-in-Publication Data
Names: Kasper, Walter, 1933– author
Title: The challenge of mercy: Christian life in today's world / Walter Kasper.
Description: Paperback. | New York: Paulist Press, [2026] | Summary: "This work has its origins with a public talk Cardinal Kasper gave in 2015"—Provided by publisher.
Identifiers: LCCN 2025048650 (print) | LCCN 2025048651 (ebook) | ISBN 9780809158010 paperback | ISBN 9780809189670 ebook
Subjects: LCSH: Mercy | Christian life—Catholic authors
Classification: LCC BV4647.M4 K37 2026 (print) | LCC BV4647.M4 (ebook)
LC record available at https://lccn.loc.gov/2025048650

LC ebook record available at https://lccn.loc.gov/2025048651

ISBN 978-0-8091-5801-0 (paperback)
ISBN 978-0-8091-8967-0 (ebook)

Published by Paulist Press
997 Macarthur Boulevard
Mahwah, New Jersey 07430
www.paulistpress.com

Printed and bound in the
United States of America

CONTENTS

PREFACE

Among the most significant and influential theologians of the past fifty years, Cardinal Walter Kasper is without doubt the one who has most deeply reflected on the difficult relationship between revelation and philosophy. Born in the "fateful" year 1933 in Heidenheim, he studied in Tübingen and Munich between 1952 and 1956; he was ordained a priest in 1957 and earned his doctorate in theology in 1961. From the early 1960s until his appointment as bishop of Rottenburg-Stuttgart in 1989, Kasper taught dogmatic theology at the faculties of Münster and Tübingen, all the while actively engaged in church life with positions of great prestige: he served as member and consultant of numerous Vatican commissions, in particular the Congregation for the Doctrine of the Faith, the Pontifical Council for Culture, and the Congregation for the Eastern Churches. In 1999, John Paul II appointed him secretary of the Pontifical Council for Promoting Christian Unity, of which he is now president emeritus. In 2001, his extraordinary prestige as both theologian and churchman was recognized in the most solemn way by his elevation to the rank of cardinal.

For Kasper, as his whole career demonstrates, theological knowledge is inseparable from the principle of ecclesiality. The universality of his Christianity is *universale concretum*, concrete universality, and must always be able to address—without any loss of rigor or coherence—concrete problems and the historicity of existence. Theology, theological discourse, is therefore intrinsically dialogical, and its interlocutor—integral to its very formation—is the real world, in its real sufferings, expectations, and hopes. Kasper's ecclesiology, in this sense, is eucharistic, entirely shaped by the idea of *communio fidelium*. No priestly exclusivism can be admitted; the letter must never prevail over the spirit. No one can fail to see the immense difficulty of this "system": faith, even as fidelity to tradition, is called to measure itself against the urgency of the present moment, to listen to it and understand it, to take the risk of engaging with it daily, and to be reborn—revived—each time through it. Nothing could be further from a negligent faith, from a faith that "assures."

Kasper has developed these themes in works pivotal for twentieth-century theology: from *Glaube und Geschichte* (1970) to *Jesus der Christus* (1974) to *Der Gott Jesu Christi* (1982) to the vast *Theologie und Kirche* (1987–1999). These works constitute perhaps the most significant development and deepening of Vatican II theology, whose influence has grown over the years and which now appear to me fundamental even for anyone wishing to interpret—in its authentic depth and not according to certain popular distortions—the reform undertaken by Pope Francis. His report for the Synod on the Family is clear testimony to this: no "compromise," but a return to the absolutely essential, making it the key for interpreting history, considered realistically, and for defining the ways in which to act within it. As a Christian, yes—but a Christian who addresses all and believes that the "measure" of his work is every possible human being.

It is evident that such a theology cannot be content with a calm, scholastic, intellectually abstract separation from philosophy. "Faith and history" means "faith and reason"—and that conjunction is as necessary as it is highly problematic. Any mutual indifference between philosophy and theology contradicts, *ab imis fundamentis*, the whole of our culture and civilization. The dialogue between the two is required for a purely "logical" reason: philosophical knowledge cannot rest content with the purely relative—any search for the gift of meaning implies, willingly or unwillingly, reference to the Absolute, at least as a problem *semper indagandum*. On the other hand, faith cannot be assumed either as a reassuring presupposition (its truth, as Thomas says, is *semper indaganda*), nor reduced to a psychological phenomenon—a presupposition of every form of "natural theology," which inevitably leads to eliminating the living historicity of the great religious messages. But—and here is the *novitas*!—whereas in other religions this historicity is in some way repudiated or considered inessential, for Christianity (and, though in radically different forms, for the other Abrahamic monotheisms) it becomes absolutely essential. The unbreakable bond between the Absolute and history is its mark—the very sign of the Cross.

It is therefore no surprise that Kasper's great interlocutor in his philosophical-theological research has, from the beginning, been Friedrich Schelling. On the fruitfulness of Schelling's philosophy—beginning with the *Philosophische Untersuchungen über das Wesen der menschlichen Freiheit* of 1809—Kasper has insisted since 1965 in a book fundamental to all studies of this author and, more generally, of the "crisis" of classical German idealism: *Das Absolute in der Geschichte: Philosophie und Theologie der Geschichte in der Spätphilosophie Schellings.* We cannot here even attempt to unfold the wealth of themes and problems this work addresses, but I wish to indicate its key idea, for it perhaps explains the real reason why this Faculty of Philosophy and this whole university so greatly desired to meet Cardinal Kasper today.

The Absolute in history bears the name of freedom. Freedom is the unconditional that is realized historically; every one of our thoughts and actions presupposes its idea, and no reason, no "calculation" or demonstration can found it. Man does not live as man without freedom, but freedom is a gift. He is called to guard and defend it; he cannot create it, nor define it as a concept. In this, Schelling criticizes Hegelian idealism and indeed meets, on essential points, authors like Søren Kierkegaard. Freedom is the supreme gift of God's own freedom; it is his image in us, the "point" where truly *abyssus abyssum vocat*. But how is being free expressed? In only one way:

by acting to liberate—liberate from servitude, from misery, from pain. Earthly happiness and blessedness have meaning only if united, only if they fulfill one another. Man is the Dasein who expresses his freedom by seeking in every way his own *Befriedigung*, the *enérgheia* of his nature. In various forms, this is the aim of all people of good will. But to hear suffering and to care for it, our freedom must be merciful. We respond responsibly to the gift of being free only by giving and forgiving.

This is the great theme—the exact counterpart to that of *Theós Agápe* developed in Pope Benedict's great encyclical—that Kasper has explored in his most recent *Barmherzigkeit*, defining *mercy* as the fundamental concept of the gospel and the key to Christian life. In the Vulgate, "mercy" translates various Greek terms: the *misericordes* of the Beatitudes are the *eleémones*; those in Luke 6:36 are the *oiktírmones* (both terms relate to the sphere of lament: *eleéō* may have an onomatopoeic root, *eu, eu*; *oîktos* means "lament"). But the strongest word for mercy is that in the parable of the Good Samaritan: the Samaritan, seeing the man wounded and abandoned, "feels mercy"—*misericordia motus est*, says the Vulgate—but in Greek the expression is even more forceful: *esplanchnísthē* (*splánchnon* means "viscera"; *plegḗ* means "blow"): the Samaritan's guts are wrenched at the sight; he cannot turn away; he must draw near. To draw near in this way—that is what it means to be merciful: to care for the other so radically as to feel oneself torn apart before his suffering, and to seek by every means to heal him—

and in so doing, to heal ourselves, our own insides that cannot bear, cannot tolerate his suffering.

You will then understand why the entire scholarly community of San Raffaele, following the inspiration of its founder, wished to have among its honorary graduates Cardinal and Professor Walter Kasper. The Faculty of Philosophy, the youngest of the university, striving to be worthy of its colleagues in medicine, psychology, and research, with their great international renown, has merely interpreted a common sentiment: that no one better than Cardinal and Professor Walter Kasper could express the essential values of the whole San Raffaele University.

This university was founded and lives for one purpose: to care—for merciful, active, concrete, scientifically organized care, capable of enduring and developing—for the human person in the harmony of all his faculties. No separateness, no body/soul dualism. We are curious—scientifically curious—about the human being in all the forms of his activity; we want to care for his body and his mind, as well as for the works this extraordinary unity of body and mind produces—for the soul it expresses by creating, acting, dialoguing, hoping, believing. All our knowledge is directed to the other, to the thing itself.

The Faculty of Philosophy's motto reads: *De nobis ipsis tacemus, de re agitur* (Of ourselves we keep silent; it is the matter itself that matters). I believe it applies to the whole university. No *philautía* or *philopsychía*, no arrogant self-sufficiency has any place in our university. And to what does the principle of mercy stand opposed, if not to the inhospitable love of self—for one's own self? This principle applies to all of us: to philosophers as to doctors, as to psychologists—indeed, to each of us as doctor-psychologist-philosopher.

Massimo Cacciari

1

MERCY

Reviving a Neglected Theme

I will speak about the theme of mercy—a theme that is central in the Bible, both in the Old and New Testaments. If one wished, the whole Gospel could be summarized under the title of mercy. Not infrequently "mercy" has become the key word of the present pontificate, and with this message Pope Francis has touched the hearts of many people, both inside and outside the Catholic Church. Who among us does not need mercy and merciful people?

All the more, then, was I surprised when, some years ago, I set out to prepare a lecture on mercy. The lecture did not want to see the light of day. I consulted theological manuals and the entries on mercy in theological dictionaries, but they were of no help to me. I thought: this cannot be true—that such a central and fundamental theme should be inexcusably neglected in systematic theology, reduced to a small subheading under "justice," and even there treated by authors who often seemed at a loss. They would ask how a God who, for them, is primarily just could also be merciful, for insofar as he is just, he must condemn and punish the wicked and reward the good. What a poor and miserable idea of God—of a God forced to act according to our rules of justice; a God who is an idol of our own conceptions, an ideological construct, an executor and prisoner of our demands for an allegedly just order! Such a God would no longer be God, but an idol turned ideology.

Very soon, however, I discovered that mercy is not only a problem of the theology found in neo-Scholastic manuals; it is also a problem in philosophy—or better, in certain philosophical currents. According to the quintessential modern philosopher, Immanuel Kant, ethics must be guided not by emotions such as mercy or compassion, but by the very awareness of moral duty. One might also think of Marxist or socialist philosophies, which suspect that mercy is a substitute for justice—a patching-up of individual potholes of social need instead of reforming the entire social system and creating a new order of justice for all. We hear the cry: "We don't want mercy—no, we want justice! We want our rights! We don't want a state or an employer to give us alms out of mercy—no, we have a right to a just wage!"

It is good that our political system is based on the ideal of justice, and for that we are grateful. But our economic and social system is also based on competition. There is no room for compassion and mercy. The one with the greatest intelligence and the most success prevails—often the strongest or the most cunning, the one able to impose his will against the interests of others without concern for them. In our society, social-Darwinist tendencies often prevail—survival of the fittest, the ruthless assertion of selfish interests.

The word of Jesus in his Sermon on the Mount—"Blessed are the merciful"—sounds strange in this context.

Finally, Friedrich Nietzsche despised mercy as an expression of weakness, unworthy of the noble (*Herrenmensch*)—the strong and the hard. In *Thus Spoke Zarathustra*, Nietzsche sketched a true counter-gospel to the Sermon on the Mount. The abuses that the Nazis made of his ideas were terrible, with their ideology of a master race and their contempt for the weak, the handicapped, and the so-called races unworthy of life.

Indeed, the two ideologies of Marxism and Nazism—both of which so devastated the twentieth century and caused so much suffering to so many people—led to a rethinking of the idea of mercy. A world without compassion and without mercy is a cold world.

There are shocking testimonies about the human misery and despair in which the atheist world of Soviet Marxism found itself, where life was lived in the total absence of mercy. We know that in the end, with mercy, justice too was lost and trampled underfoot.

Already Pope John XXIII, in his opening address to the Second Vatican Council, said: "Today the Church prefers to use the medicine of mercy rather than that of severity." The future Pope John Paul II had lived through the terror of the Second World War, the Nazi dictatorship, and the communist dictatorship in Poland—a situation marked by injustice, the absence of rights, and the absence of mercy. In such circumstances, he rediscovered the importance of biblical mercy and issued the second encyclical of his pontificate precisely on the theme of mercy, *Dives in misericordia* (1980). As a response to the terrors of the last century, Pope Benedict deepened this message in his encyclical *Deus caritas est* (2005).

Now Pope Francis has made mercy the central and fundamental theme of his pontificate. This also springs from personal experience. In the slums of Buenos Aires, he encountered people who felt themselves to be, and were treated as, refuse—men and women, children and the elderly excluded from economic and cultural progress; street children, often abused. Even today there is talk of at least twelve million slaves worldwide—human beings forced to live in miserable conditions and compelled to perform forced labor. And who among us does not think of the fate of millions exposed to brutal and cynical terrorism, of refugees in the hands of traffickers without conscience? The theme of mercy is not outdated; the message of mercy is of pressing relevance.

2

FIRST APPROACHES TO MERCY

The contemporary urgency of mercy invites us to dig into the tradition of human thought for a response to our present situation. Although the word *mercy* is specific to the Bible and the biblical tradition, its preparations and anticipations can be found in the human tradition of the West. The philosophical tradition—and even the theory of tragedy in the West—knows compassion. Classical tragedy requires the spectator to experience compassion for the fate of the hero, and in him, to see his own fate. From there, in the modern theory of theater, often came an interest in the moral education of the spectator.

Empathy (*Einfühlung*) and sympathy are thus constitutive of the humanistic tradition.

In almost all religions of humanity we find the so-called Golden Rule: “What you do not want done to yourself, do not do to another,” or in its positive formulation: “What you want done to yourself, do also to another.” This Golden Rule is a heritage of all humanity. It is a rule of empathy that asks us to go beyond our own self, to put ourselves in the other’s situation, and to act as we would wish the other to act toward us in such a situation.

These examples reveal an anthropology that is not self-referential or closed in on itself, but an anthropology of the human being who must open to the other—a human being defined by *empáthein* and *sympáthein* with the other, and by a self-understanding that comes from the other, toward the other, and in the other.

The biblical tradition—as we will soon see—goes further. It is worth adding already, however, that the Qur’an, to a certain extent, participates in the biblical tradition. Every surah of the Qur’an (with one exception) begins with the invocation of Almighty and All-Merciful Allah. There are, therefore, similarities with the biblical conception of mercy—similarities that are important for interreligious dialogue and for Islam’s self-understanding, which contradicts terrorism. Yet precisely where the similarity appears, the decisive dissimilarity between the Bible and the Qur’an also emerges. The conception of Allah as God is not the same as that of YHWH in the Old Testament or of the God and Father of Jesus. A God who, out of mercy, lowers himself to the point of becoming man and dying on the cross is utterly unimaginable for Islam; indeed, it is strongly rejected as being in strict contradiction with the absolute transcendence of God.

Thus, even at this point, it becomes clear that with the idea of mercy we touch not only the conception of the human being as a being with and for others, but also the specifically Judeo-Christian conception of God himself. In mercy, we encounter the very identity of Christianity.

3

MERCY IN THE OLD TESTAMENT

If we open the Bible, we find already in its first pages that God created everything in goodness, but through sin, chaos entered the world. In the first chapters of the Bible, we do not often find the word *mercy*. Yet from the very beginning we see that God resists evil and chaos. After the flood, he guarantees the order of the world and grants humanity a space for life and survival (cf. Gen 8–9). God wills life and protects life; even after sin, he grants a new beginning, a new chance. The same is true after the disaster of the tower of Babel, with the scattering and division of humanity. With Abraham, God began a new story and a new gathering together of the whole human family. The blessing given to Abraham was a blessing for all nations: "In you all the [nations] shall be blessed" (Gen 12:3; 18:18; 22:18; 28:14, passim). Here again, the term *mercy* is not yet present, but the reality of mercy is already there. God does not will death but life; he never abandons his creature; he will never abandon humanity. God always offers a new chance.

A new stage in salvation history appears with Moses and the liberation of Israel from Egypt. God reveals himself to Moses in the burning bush as the God who hears the cry of his people and sees their misery. Notice: God hears, God sees; his heart is with his people (cf. Exod 3:7ff). His name, which he reveals to Moses—YHWH—is translated in the Septuagint and the Vulgate as "I am who I am" (*ho ōn*; Exod 3:14). From this translation arose the entire doctrine of God and the metaphysical concept of God as Absolute Being. This concept is not wrong. In truth, however, the original meaning of YHWH is deeper: "I am and will be present; I am and will be with you; I am your God, and you are my people" (cf. Exod 6:7). In his name, God shows compassion, deep feeling, readiness to help. God is the God-with-his-people. He is the God who walks with his people and accompanies them on the journey of their history. He is the God who frees his people.

In a second revelation, God says to Moses: "I will be gracious to whom I will be gracious, and will show mercy on whom I will show mercy" (Exod 33:19). Mercy, then, is not merely an expression of goodwill, but of sovereignty, freedom, independence, and lordship. The metaphysical meaning is implicitly present, but the biblical meaning is more dynamic and personal. Because God is God, he is merciful. Because God is absolute, he is merciful. Mercy is his absolute being.

A third aspect appears in the third revelation to Moses: "The Lord, a God merciful and gracious, slow to anger, and abounding in steadfast love and faithfulness" (Exod 34:6). Now mercy is not only an expression of sovereignty and freedom, but also of God's faithfulness. We can rely on him in every situation. In the Bible, this formula from the third revelation is regarded as God's name and almost as a definition of his essence. For this reason, in the Old Testament, especially in the Psalms, it is constantly repeated (cf. Deut 4:31; Ps 86:15; 103:8; 116:5; 145:8; passim).

The summit of the Old Testament revelation of God's mercy is found in the prophet Hosea. He lived and worked in a dramatic situation, and the drama of his message corresponds to it. The people had broken the covenant and become an "unfaithful prostitute." Therefore God broke with his people and decided to show no more mercy to the faithless nation. His people are not, and will not be, his people (cf. Hos 1:6–9). The covenant seems entirely ended, with no future in sight. Then comes the dramatic reversal: "My heart recoils within me" (Hos 11:8). More accurately, God overturns his own justice, so to speak, casting it aside. The place of annihilating wrath is taken by an upheaval within God himself. His compassion bursts forth, and in him mercy prevails over justice. The motive for this upheaval reveals the very depth of the divine mystery: "For I am God and no mortal, the Holy One in your midst, and I will not come in wrath" (Hos 11:9).

This astonishing affirmation means: God's holiness—his being totally other than anything human—is not manifested in just anger, nor in inaccessible and unfathomable transcendence. God's being is revealed in his mercy. Mercy is the expression of his divine essence. It is what completely distinguishes him from human beings and raises him above all that is human. It is his loftiness and his sovereignty. The prophet Micah says: "He delights in showing clemency" (Mic 7:18).

The Old Testament, then, is not—as many suspect—merely a message of justice, vengeance, and God's wrath. It already prepares the message of Jesus and the New Testament on the mercy of God.

4

MERCY IN THE NEW TESTAMENT

At the center of Jesus's message is the proclamation of God as *Abba*, Father. One need only recall Jesus's beautiful parable of the prodigal son—which should more rightly be called the parable of the merciful father (cf. Luke 15:11–32). It is moving: the father waits for the son and runs out to meet him. God waits, God comes to meet us, embraces us, and restores to his prodigal son all his rights as a child.

Most of all, God has come to meet us in the mission of his only Son, who humbled himself and became human even to death on a cross (cf. Phil 2:5–11). The Crucified One is the concrete image of God's mercy. We can also recall the parable of the Good Samaritan, which has become proverbial even beyond Christian and ecclesial circles (cf. Luke 10:25–37). This parable shows a reversal, a true change of perspective: to the question "Who is my neighbor?" Jesus does not answer with deductions from lofty principles, but imagines the situation of a man who suffers and can no longer help himself—a man whom I find and encounter on the road. This suffering man embodies God's concrete will for me.

It would be mistaken to interpret the parable merely as a message of universal humanism. It illustrates the behavior of Jesus, which in turn is the manifestation of God's behavior, and of him who could say of himself: "I am gentle and humble in heart" (Matt 11:29).

At the end, Jesus sacrificed his life "to give his life as a ransom for many," that is, for each and all of us (cf. Mark 10:45; 1 Tim 2:6). This vicarious death of Christ—remembered and made present each time in the celebration of the Eucharist—is not only a sign of solidarity with us, not merely a moral reality. There is also the deeper, metaphysical need: the destiny of death, which raises the question of the meaning of our life. Through sin we have earned death (cf. Gen 2:17; Rom 5:12). We cannot free ourselves from death. Only God, Lord of life and death, can come to our aid and free us. In Jesus, God himself, in his mercy, took our place. As God, death could not hold him. By his death, he destroyed death, and life has triumphed. Jesus Christ gave his life so that we might live.

The justification of the sinner—the great theme of Luther and the Reformation, often misunderstood today—means this: normally the guilty must be condemned to death, but thanks to God's mercy, we are sentenced to life. We are acquitted, freed from death, and called to Christian freedom (cf. Gal 5:1). Thus the message of mercy touches the very heart of theology and soteriology, and we can also say, it touches the very center of our human and Christian existence. In no human situation—not even in the situation of our death—can we fall deeper than into the hands of the merciful God. The Letter to the Ephesians sums it up in the words: "God...is rich in mercy" (Eph 2:4).

5

MERCY, THE NAME OF OUR GOD

As we have already seen from the beginning, mercy touches the question of God himself. And the question of God concerns the deepest crisis of our time—and is also its most important question. Although atheism and agnosticism were already present in certain philosophers of the past, mass atheism and mass agnosticism are a recent phenomenon of secularized Western civilization. Throughout the earlier history of humanity, there was never a culture without religion.

The Second Vatican Council stated that atheism, in its various forms, is one of the most serious problems of our age, but it also added that Christians themselves bear some responsibility for it. The Council observed that we have often obscured the image of God. Too often we have proclaimed a one-sided image of the just God who punishes, and at times we have even portrayed a God of vengeance—while underestimating the message of the merciful God, who in his mercy does not will the death of the sinner but life. We have overburdened the image of the living God—who walks with his people and is present in every situation—with speculative ideas about God's immutability. These are not wrong in themselves, but when understood one-sidedly, they have distanced God from life.

The Bible tells us: "God is love" (1 John 4:8)—that is, self-communication. Above all, God is the self-communication of love within the Trinity. God is not a solitary God; the Trinitarian God is communion. The outward expression of this inner love and communication is mercy. Mercy is God's fidelity to himself, who is love. Because God is faithful to himself, he wills to communicate his being—first in creation, then in salvation history. He cannot but forgive and give a new chance to every sinner who repents and converts.

Thus, mercy becomes the mirror of the Trinity and, according to St. Thomas Aquinas, the first and greatest attribute of God. In his mercy, God opens his heart and allows us to see into it. When I gave Pope Francis my book on mercy—just a few days after its publication in Spanish translation—he said to me: "Mercy, that is the name of our God!"

The statement "God is mercy" means that God has a heart for the wretched. He is not a God "up in the clouds," uninterested in the fate of human beings, but one who is moved and touched by human misery. He is a compassionate God, a "sympathetic" (in the original sense of the word) God.

These and similar considerations have led contemporary theology to reexamine the immutability and impassibility of God. It is and remains true that God is always the same, without change or development. God is not, in a passive sense, touched by evil; in that sense, there is no passion or suffering in God. But because of his sovereign freedom in love, in an active and deliberate sense, he allows himself to be moved and touched by human misery. There is no passion in God, but there is compassion in God.

Here we come to the deepest problems of theology: God and evil, God and innocent suffering, God and the injustice and wickedness in the world—problems that challenge us, whether in the Shoah of the twentieth century or in the unprecedented brutalities of our own twenty-first. A theoretical answer in the sense of traditional theodicy—such as Gottfried Wilhelm von Leibniz attempted—seems to me impossible. We cannot imagine a theory that would explain or "solve" the mysteries of God and of the suffering person—who can never be reduced to a theory or an ideology.

The answer cannot be theoretical; it must be practical. The question is a challenge to our own mercy. We must bring at least a faint ray of divine mercy into the darkness of the world.

6

MERCY

Key to Christian Existence in Society

To believe in this God of mercy is not to believe merely that a God exists somewhere—perhaps somewhere above the clouds. No: if the merciful God exists, that changes my whole life! The fundamental biblical principle for the Christian's life is: "Be imitators of God" (Eph 5:1). We are called to imitate God. In this sense Jesus says: "Be perfect...as your heavenly Father is perfect" (Matt 5:48). The evangelist Luke gives what is probably the original wording: "Be merciful, just as your Father is merciful" (Luke 6:36).

In this same spirit, the first and greatest commandment—the love of God and love of neighbor—are inseparably united (cf. Matt 22:34–40). No one can love God without also loving his neighbor (cf. 1 John 4:20; 3:10–18).

Here lies the heart of the Sermon on the Mount: "Blessed are the merciful" (Matt 5:7). In his discourse on the Last Judgment, Jesus recognizes only one criterion: how we have acted toward the hungry, the thirsty, the naked, the sick, the imprisoned. Jesus will not ask us whether we have kept the sixth commandment. Certainly, that commandment is also important, since it too refers to respect for others—that is, to true love, which is something different from mere pleasure or the satisfaction of one's desires. Yet only love and mercy will be decisive. Love and mercy will be the only things we can carry with us and present before the judgment of Jesus. For in the poor we meet Jesus himself, and he will recognize us when we meet him (cf. Matt 25:31–46).

Christian tradition lists seven corporal works of mercy and seven spiritual works of mercy. The corporal works are: to feed the hungry, give drink to the thirsty, clothe the naked, welcome the stranger, visit the sick, visit the imprisoned, and bury the dead. Some of these are especially timely: feeding and giving drink call us to justice in a world where the resources of life are so unjustly distributed; welcoming the stranger becomes a matter of conscience in the face of millions of refugees—a true sign of the times; visiting the sick and elderly is ever more important in a society that values only those who are young, healthy, strong, and successful, while the number of elderly people living alone grows; visiting the imprisoned means improving and humanizing their situation, and working for those unjustly detained (political prisoners, prisoners for reasons of religion, and—never to be forgotten—persecuted Christians).

All the realism of Christianity comes to light when we turn to the spiritual works of mercy. For there is not only material poverty, but also cultural poverty—such as that of those who have no access to education (think of the problem of illiteracy); relational poverty, the poverty of communication in loneliness; and, not least, spiritual poverty—the inner emptiness and growing desert of the heart, the lack and loss of orientation in life. In this sense, the spiritual works of mercy become strikingly relevant again: to instruct the ignorant, counsel the doubtful, comfort the afflicted, admonish sinners, forgive offenses, bear with those who are difficult (often the hardest task of all), and pray for everyone.

These works of mercy—both corporal and spiritual—are by no means intended to replace the order of a just society. The idea of a social state that guarantees a human life worthy of the human person has existed since the nineteenth century, because poverty is not only an individual problem but also a social evil and dysfunction. We have every reason to preserve and improve our social system.

Yet its limits must also be recognized. Need takes many forms and often changes rapidly. It is impossible to regulate and anticipate every individual situation, and those who try to do so end up creating a bureaucratic system full of rules, through whose meshes people will always slip—so that, as the Romans already said, *summum ius* becomes *summa iniuria* ("the highest law becomes the greatest injustice"). Bureaucratization of the social and health sectors—unavoidable to a certain extent—often creates new problems and ends in a cold, impersonal, and anonymous system. For example, illness is not only a problem of a particular organ, but of the whole person—an emotional and existential problem. The patient needs professional help, but also empathy and sympathy in the original sense of the word: he needs mercy, a heart for the wretched. A comforting and encouraging word often replaces medicine and, because of the psychosomatic unity of the person, can prove to be the best medicine.

The problem is made worse by the growing commercialization of health and social services. And we have not yet even touched on many future challenges—such as the demographic question: how will a smaller and smaller number of young people care for, both personally and economically, a greater and greater number of elderly people who, thanks to medical progress, live longer and require longer and more expensive care?

Faced with such problems, mercy and the works of mercy show their relevance not only in particular situations but in a more general sense. Social order cannot survive without the personal and private initiative of individuals within the family, neighborhood, and voluntary service. But this requires motivation—it requires mercy, a heart (*cor*) for the wretched, a heart open with open hands and feet ready to move to help those in need. Personal mercy does not wish to replace social justice, but can be its inspiration and motivation.

We need people who perceive the need that often arises unexpectedly, who allow themselves to be moved by it—people with a heart, who take others to heart and, in concrete cases, try to help as best they can. Without such mercy, the motivational basis for the further development of social legislation is lost. Our society cannot manage without mercy. Today, in the face of the enormous problems we must confront, without a religious foundation the emotional impulse needed to work for a better world is lacking. Without mercy, our society risks becoming a desert. We can, therefore, understand mercy as the foundation, the innovative source, and the motivational force of social justice. Mercy—though it is a supernatural virtue—has its natural reasonableness and urgency.

This must be compared with Jesus's strongest commandment: "As God forgives us seventy times seven, so we must also forgive and love even our enemies" (cf. Matt 5:43–44; 18:21–22). Sigmund Freud said that the commandment to love one's enemy is absurd because it is impossible. Certainly, it is not easy, and often it requires a long journey to be able to forgive and love an enemy. But this is what God has done with us. And only in this way has he broken the vicious circle in which every injustice causes vengeance, and vengeance causes new injustice, and so on. Mercy breaks this vicious circle and allows for a new beginning—a new common path toward the future. Mercy that extends even to the forgiveness of the enemy is certainly not easy, yet it is not absurd; it is reasonable. Only through mercy and forgiveness can we be peacemakers (cf. Matt 5:9).

This was the wisdom of the great Italian, French, and German statesmen after the disaster of the Second World War: from enemy peoples they became friendly nations. Thus were laid the foundations of peace and the future of Europe—and we must hope that today national selfishness and irrational resentments from the past will not prevail again, so that Europe's peace and future may endure.

7

THE CHURCH

Sacrament of Mercy

Finally, let us speak of the ecclesial dimension of mercy. The Second Vatican Council described the Church as, in a sense, a sacrament of Christ—that is, a sign and instrument of Christ. Thus, the Church is also a sacrament—sign and instrument—of Christ's mercy. In its visible, social, and institutional dimension, it must represent and make visible the merciful Christ.

From this perspective we understand the scandal that the Church is sometimes perceived as—and even accused of—being not merciful, but harsh and severe. It was precisely because of his spiritual insight that Pope John XXIII said in his famous opening address to the council:

> There is no time in which the Church has not opposed these errors; frequently she has also

> condemned them, and at times with the greatest severity. As regards the present time, the Bride of Christ prefers to make use of the medicine of mercy rather than to arm herself with the weapons of severity. She thinks that she meets the needs of the present day by demonstrating the validity of her teaching more fully rather than by condemning.

With these words, the pope set in motion not only the council, but also the post-conciliar pastoral orientation. Pope Paul VI confirmed this choice and carried it forward. In his final address to the council, he said that the behavior of the Good Samaritan is the spirituality of the council. Pope John Paul II published his second encyclical on mercy, as we have already seen. Pope Francis, in *Evangelii gaudium*, is in perfect continuity with the council and his predecessors: *mercy* is the key word of his pontificate.

The Church has a threefold mission regarding mercy: to proclaim mercy, to celebrate mercy in the liturgy of the sacraments—especially in the sacrament of mercy, the sacrament of penance, and in the eucharistic liturgy—and to practice mercy in her pastoral life. Pastoral mercy must not be confused with a pseudo-mercy, that is, with a pastoral practice of mere indulgence and a "light" Christianity available on the cheap.

Mercy itself is the fundamental truth of the Christian faith. Therefore, it cannot be opposed to the witness of the truth. Theologically, it is entirely senseless to set it against the truth or to suspect that it might weaken other truths or God's commandments, or dispense from conversion. On the contrary, as the fundamental truth according to the hierarchy of truths, mercy must be understood as the hermeneutical principle for interpreting and applying the truths of faith and for interpreting and applying canon law, whose supreme law is the salvation of souls. In this way, mercy continually makes the beauty of the Gospel and the faith shine forth—never out of date, always timely, always new, and always surprising.

In mercy, the Church presents herself as a merciful mother, whose home is always open to her children—a Church with open doors, not closed drawbridges. In this context I will not enter into concrete pastoral problems or complex situations—such as the question of divorced and remarried persons, discussed controversially during last October's Extraordinary Synod. I am convinced that in the Ordinary Synod scheduled for October of this year, a broad consensus will be reached, just as at the Second Vatican Council, whose fiftieth anniversary of conclusion we celebrate this year. That Council had many long debates and controversies, but in the end it always reached a broad consensus well beyond the required two-thirds majority. I believe the same will happen this time.

Here I want to point only to the deepest dimension of mercy. It has not only a social and ecclesial dimension, but also a Christological and mystical one. Jesus came to proclaim the Gospel—the good news to the poor (cf. Luke 4:18). He who was rich became poor and weak even to the cross (cf. 2 Cor 8:9). This *kenosis*—this self-emptying, this self-stripping and self-humbling—continues in his mystical body, the Church; it continues in the poor. Pope Francis often repeats that in the wounds of the battered and the poor we can touch Jesus himself; what we have done for the poor and the wretched, we have done for him (cf. Matt 25:40).

This Christological and mystical aspect of mercy is very dear to Pope Francis. His program is deeply rooted in the biblical tradition and in the tradition of the saints. St. Benedict admonishes monks to welcome a stranger as Christ himself. St. Francis of Assisi, at the beginning of his spiritual journey, embraced and kissed a leper. Mother Teresa received her original vocation when, on the streets of Calcutta, she found a dying man, carried him into her convent, and felt she was carrying Christ himself in her hands. The Second Vatican Council rediscovered this dimension in its dogmatic constitution on the Church. With his teaching, Pope Francis follows an ancient tradition and begins a new phase of the reception of the council.

At the same time, this teaching speaks directly to the present situation of the world, where more than two thirds of humanity—including many Christians—live in poverty and misery, while in the Western world we live in a society of abundance. The social gulf between rich and poor is widening, and above all the spiritual desert is growing—where many ask: How can I find and encounter Christ in this deeply secularized world?

In this situation, mercy and its spirituality become

the key to Christian existence. Its mysticism is not that of closed, but of open eyes—eyes that lead us to open hearts, open hands, and swift feet to go out to meet those in need and in misery. Thus, mercy becomes fundamental for a spirituality and mysticism not only for monastics and clergy, but for a lay mysticism lived in the midst of the world.

Appendix

Mercy in the Words of Recent Popes

Pope John XXIII

FROM OPENING ADDRESS, SECOND VATICAN COUNCIL, OCTOBER 11, 1962

As for the present time, the bride of Christ prefers to use the medicine of mercy instead of taking up the weapons of rigor; she thinks that one should meet today's needs, by exposing more clearly the value of her teaching rather than by condemning. Not because there is a lack of false doctrines, opinions, dangers to guard against and to oppose; but because all of them contrast so openly with the right principles of honesty, and have produced such lethal fruits that today men seem to begin spontaneously to reprobate them, especially those forms of existence that ignore God and His laws, placing too much trust in the progress of technology, basing well-being solely on the comforts of life. They are increasingly aware that the dignity of the human person and his natural perfection is a matter of great importance and very difficult to achieve. What matters above all is that they have learned through experience that external violence exercised on others, the power of weapons, political domination are absolutely not enough to resolve for the best the very serious problems that torment them.

This being so, the Catholic Church, while raising the torch of Catholic truth with this ecumenical council, wishes to show herself to be a most loving mother to all, benign, patient, moved by mercy and goodness toward her separated children. To humanity troubled by so many difficulties she says, as Peter did to the poor man who had asked him for alms: "Of silver and gold I have no possessions, but what I have I give you: in the name of Jesus Christ of Nazareth, walk!" (*Acts* 3:6).

In other words, the Church does not offer the men of our times perishable riches, nor does it promise merely earthly happiness; but it dispenses the goods of supernatural grace, which, by elevating the men to the dignity of children of God, are such a valid defense and help to make their life more human; it opens the sources of its most fruitful doctrine, with which men, enlightened by the light of Christ, succeed in understanding deeply what they really are, what dignity they are invested with, to what goal they must tend; finally, through its children it manifests everywhere the greatness of Christian charity, than which nothing is more effective in uprooting the seeds of discord, nothing more effective in promoting harmony, just peace and fraternal union of all.

Pope Paul VI

FROM CLOSING ADDRESS, SECOND VATICAN COUNCIL, DECEMBER 7, 1965

The Church of the council has been concerned, not just with herself and with her relationship of union with God, but with man—man as he really is today: living man, man all wrapped up in himself, man who makes himself not only the center of his every interest but dares to claim that he is the principle and explanation of all reality. Every perceptible element in man, every one of the countless guises in which he appears, has, in a sense, been displayed in full view of the council Fathers, who, in their turn, are mere men, and yet all of them are pastors and brothers whose position accordingly fills them with solicitude and love. Among these guises we may cite man as the tragic actor of his own plays; man as the superman of yesterday and today, ever frail, unreal, selfish, and savage; man unhappy with himself as he laughs and cries; man the versatile actor ready to perform any part; man the narrow devotee of nothing but scientific reality; man as he is, a creature who thinks and loves and toils and is always waiting for something, the "growing son" (Gen. 49:22); man sacred because of the innocence of his childhood, because of the mystery of his poverty, because of the dedication of his suffering; man as an individual and man in society; man who lives in the glories of the past and dreams of those of the future; man the sinner and man the saint, and so on.

Secular humanism, revealing itself in its horrible anti-clerical reality has, in a certain sense, defied the council. The religion of the God who became man has met the religion (for such it is) of man who makes himself God. And what happened? Was there a clash, a battle, a condemnation? There could have been, but there was none. The old story of the Samaritan has been the model of the spirituality of the council. A feeling of boundless sympathy has permeated the whole of it. The attention of our council has been absorbed by the discovery of human needs (and these needs grow in proportion to the greatness which the son of the earth claims for himself). But we call upon those who term themselves modern humanists, and who have renounced the transcendent value of the highest realities, to give the council credit at least for one quality and to recognize our own new type of humanism: we, too, in fact, we more than any others, honor mankind.

And what aspect of humanity has this august senate studied? What goal under divine inspiration did it set for itself? It also dwelt upon humanity's ever twofold facet, namely, man's wretchedness and his greatness, his profound weakness—which is undeniable and cannot be cured by himself—and the good that survives in him which is ever marked by a hidden beauty and an invincible serenity. But one must realize that this council, which exposed itself to human judgment, insisted very much more upon this pleasant side of man, rather than on his unpleasant one. Its attitude was very much and deliberately optimistic. A wave of affection and admiration flowed from the council over the modern world of humanity. Errors were condemned, indeed, because charity demanded this no less than did truth, but for the persons themselves there was only warning, respect and love. Instead of depressing diagnoses, encouraging remedies; instead of direful prognostics, messages of trust issued from the council to the present-day world. The modern world's values were not only respected but honored, its efforts approved, its aspirations purified and blessed.

You see, for example, how the countless different languages of peoples existing today were admitted for the liturgical expression of men's communication with God and God's communication with men: to man as such was recognized his fundamental claim to enjoy full possession of his rights and to his transcendental destiny. His supreme aspirations to life, to personal dignity, to his just liberty, to culture, to the renewal of the social order, to justice and peace were purified and promoted; and to all men was addressed the pastoral and missionary invitation to the light of the Gospel.

We can now speak only too briefly on the very many and vast questions, relative to human welfare, with which the council dealt. It did not attempt to resolve all the urgent problems of modern life; some of these have been reserved for a further study which the Church intends to make of them, many of them were presented in very restricted and general terms, and for that reason are open to further investigation and various applications.

But one thing must be noted here, namely, that the teaching authority of the Church, even though not wishing to issue extraordinary dogmatic pronouncements, has made thoroughly known its authoritative teaching on a number of questions which today weigh upon man's conscience and activity, descending, so to speak, into a dialogue with him, but ever preserving its own authority and force; it has spoken with the accommodating friendly voice of pastoral charity; its desire has been to be heard and understood by everyone; it has not merely concentrated on intellectual understanding but has also sought to express itself in simple, up-to-date, conversational style, derived from actual experience and a cordial approach which make it more vital, attractive and persuasive; it has spoken to modern man as he is.

Another point we must stress is this: all this rich teaching is channeled in one direction, the service of mankind, of every condition, in every weakness and need. The Church has, so to say, declared herself the servant of humanity, at the very time when her teaching role and her pastoral government have, by reason of the council's solemnity, assumed greater splendor and vigor: the idea of service has been central.

It might be said that all this and everything else we might say about the human values of the council have diverted the attention of the Church in council to the trend of modern culture, centered on humanity. We would say not diverted but rather directed. Any careful observer of the council's prevailing interest for human and temporal values cannot deny that it is from the pastoral character that the council has virtually made its program, and must recognize that the same interest is never divorced from the most genuine religious interest, whether by reason of charity, its sole inspiration (where charity is, God is!), or the council's constant, explicit attempts to link human and temporal values with those that are specifically spiritual, religious and everlasting; its concern is with man and with earth, but it rises to the kingdom of God.

The modern mind, accustomed to assess everything in terms of usefulness, will readily admit that the council's value is great if only because everything has been referred to human usefulness. Hence no one should ever say that a religion like the Catholic religion is without use, seeing that when it has its greatest self-awareness and effectiveness, as it has in council, it declares itself entirely on the side of man and in his service. In this way the Catholic religion and human life reaffirm their alliance with one another, the fact that they converge on one single human reality: the Catholic religion is for mankind. In a certain sense it is the life of mankind. It is so by the extremely precise and sublime interpretation that our religion gives of humanity (surely man by himself is a mystery to himself) and gives this interpretation in virtue of its knowledge of God: a knowledge of God is a prerequisite for a knowledge of man as he really is, in all his fullness; for proof of this let it suffice for now to recall the ardent expression of St. Catherine of Siena, "In your nature, Eternal God, I shall know my own." The Catholic religion is man's life because it determines life's nature and destiny; it gives life its real meaning, it establishes the supreme law of life and infuses it with that mysterious activity which we may say divinizes it.

Consequently, if we remember, venerable brothers and all of you, our children, gathered here, how in everyone we can and must recognize the countenance of Christ (cf. Matt. 25:40), the Son of Man, especially when tears and sorrows make it plain to see, and if we can and must recognize in Christ's countenance the countenance of our heavenly Father "He who sees me," Our Lord said, "sees also the Father" (John 14:9), our humanism becomes Christianity, our Christianity becomes centered on God; in such sort that we may say, to put it differently:

a knowledge of man is a prerequisite for a knowledge of God.

Would not this council, then, which has concentrated principally on man, be destined to propose again to the world of today the ladder leading to freedom and consolation? Would it not be, in short, a simple, new and solemn teaching to love man in order to love God? To love man, we say, not as a means but as the first step toward the final and transcendent goal which is the basis and cause of every love.

Pope John Paul II

FROM *DIVES IN MISERICORDIA*

Especially through His lifestyle and through His actions, Jesus revealed that love is present in the world in which we live—an effective love, a love that addresses itself to man and embraces everything that makes up his humanity. This love makes itself particularly noticed in contact with suffering, injustice and poverty—in contact with the whole historical "human condition," which in various ways manifests man's limitation and frailty, both physical and moral. It is precisely the mode and sphere in which love manifests itself that in biblical language is called "mercy."

Christ, then, reveals God who is Father, who is "love," as St. John will express it in his first letter; Christ reveals God as "rich in mercy," as we read in St. Paul. This truth is not just the subject of a teaching; it is a reality made present to us by Christ. Making the Father present as love and mercy is, in Christ's own consciousness, the fundamental touchstone of His mission as the Messiah;

this is confirmed by the words that He uttered first in the synagogue at Nazareth and later in the presence of His disciples and of John the Baptist's messengers.

On the basis of this way of manifesting the presence of God who is Father, love and mercy, Jesus makes mercy one of the principal themes of His preaching. As is His custom, He first teaches "in parables," since these express better the very essence of things. It is sufficient to recall the parable of the prodigal son, or the parable of the Good Samaritan, but also—by contrast—the parable of the merciless servant. There are many passages in the teaching of Christ that manifest love-mercy under some ever-fresh aspect. We need only consider the Good Shepherd who goes in search of the lost sheep, or the woman who sweeps the house in search of the lost coin. The Gospel writer who particularly treats of these themes in Christ's teaching is Luke, whose Gospel has earned the title of "the Gospel of mercy."

When one speaks of preaching, one encounters a problem of major importance with reference to the meaning of terms and the content of concepts, especially the content of the concept of "mercy" (in relationship to the concept of "love"). A grasp of the content of these concepts is the key to understanding the very reality of mercy. And this is what is most important for us. However, before devoting a further part of our considerations to this subject, that is to say, to establishing the meaning of the vocabulary and the content proper to the concept of mercy," we must note that Christ, in revealing the love—mercy of God, at the same time demanded from people that they also should be guided in their lives by love and mercy. This requirement forms part of the very essence of the messianic message, and constitutes the heart of the Gospel ethos. The Teacher expresses this both through the medium of the commandment which He describes as "the greatest," and also in the form of a blessing, when in the Sermon on the Mount He proclaims: "Blessed are the merciful, for they shall obtain mercy."

In this way, the messianic message about mercy preserves a particular divine-human dimension. Christ—the very fulfillment of the messianic prophecy—by becoming the incarnation of the love that is manifested with particular force with regard to the suffering, the unfortunate and sinners, makes present and thus more fully reveals the Father, who is God "rich in mercy." At the same time, by becoming for people a model of merciful love for others, Christ proclaims by His actions even more than by His words that call to mercy which is one of the essential elements of the Gospel ethos. In this instance it is not just a case of fulfilling a commandment or an obligation of an ethical nature; it is also a case of satisfying a condition of major importance for God to reveal Himself in His mercy to man: "The merciful...shall obtain mercy."

....

In the eschatological fulfillment mercy will be revealed as love, while in the temporal phase, in human history, which is at the same time the history of sin and death, love must be revealed above all as mercy and must also be actualized as mercy. Christ's messianic program, the program of mercy, becomes the program of His people, the program of the Church. At its very center there is always the cross, for it is in the cross that the revelation of merciful love attains its culmination. Until "the former things pass away," the cross will remain the point of reference for other words too of the Revelation of John: "Behold, I stand at the door and knock; if anyone hears my voice and opens the door, I will come in and eat with him and he with me." In a special way, God also reveals His mercy when He invites man to have "mercy" on His only Son, the crucified one.

Christ, precisely as the crucified one, is the Word that does not pass away, and He is the one who stands at the door and knocks at the heart of every man, without restricting his freedom, but instead seeking to draw from this very freedom love, which is not only an act of solidarity with the suffering Son of man, but also a kind of "mercy" shown by each one of us to the Son of the eternal Father. In the whole of this messianic program of Christ, in the whole revelation of mercy through the cross, could man's dignity be more highly respected and ennobled, for, in obtaining mercy, He is in a sense the one who at the same time "shows mercy"? In a word, is not this the position of Christ with regard to man when He says: "As you did it to one of the least of these...you did it to me"? Do not the words of the Sermon on the Mount: "Blessed are the merciful, for they shall obtain mercy," constitute, in a certain sense, a synthesis of the whole of the Good News, of the whole of the "wonderful exchange" (admirable commercium) contained therein? This exchange is a law of the very plan of salvation, a law which is simple, strong and at the same time "easy." Demonstrating from the very start what the "human heart" is capable of ("to be merciful"), do not these words from the Sermon on the Mount reveal in the same perspective the deep mystery of God: that inscrutable unity of Father, Son and Holy Spirit, in which love, containing justice, sets in motion mercy, which in its turn reveals the perfection of justice?

The Paschal Mystery is Christ at the summit of the revelation of the inscrutable mystery of God. It is precisely then that the words pronounced in the Upper Room are completely fulfilled: "He who has seen me has seen the Father." In fact, Christ, whom the Father "did not spare" for the sake of man and who in His passion and in the torment of the cross did not obtain human mercy, has revealed in His resurrection the fullness of the love that the Father has for Him and, in Him, for all people. "He is not God of the dead, but of the living." In His resurrection Christ has revealed the God of merciful love, precisely because He accepted the cross as the way to the resurrection. And it is for this reason that—when we recall the cross of Christ, His passion and death—our faith and hope are centered on the Risen One: on that Christ who "on the evening of that day, the first day of the week,...stood among them" in the upper Room, "where the disciples were,...breathed on them, and said to them: 'Receive the Holy Spirit. If you forgive the sins of any, they are forgiven; if you retain the sins of any, they are retained.'"

Here is the Son of God, who in His resurrection experienced in a radical way mercy shown to Himself, that is to say the love of the Father which is more powerful than death. And it is also the same Christ, the Son of God, who at the end of His messianic mission—and, in a certain sense, even beyond the end—reveals Himself as the inexhaustible source of mercy, of the same love that, in a subsequent perspective of the history of salvation in the Church, is to be everlastingly confirmed as more powerful than sin. The paschal Christ is the definitive incarnation of mercy, its living sign in salvation history and in eschatology. In the same spirit, the liturgy of Eastertide places on our lips the words of the Psalm: Misericordias Domini in aeternum cantabo.

Pope Benedict XVI

FROM *DEUS CARITAS EST*, DECEMBER 25, 2005

In surrounding cultures, the image of God and of the gods ultimately remained unclear and contradictory. In the development of biblical faith, however, the content of the prayer fundamental to Israel, the *Shema*, became increasingly clear and unequivocal: "Hear, O Israel, the Lord our God is one Lord" (*Dt* 6:4). There is only one God, the Creator of heaven and earth, who is thus the God of all. Two facts are significant about this statement: all other gods are not God, and the universe in which we live has its source in God and was created by him. Certainly, the notion of creation is found elsewhere, yet only here does it become absolutely clear that it is not one god among many, but the one true God himself who is the source of all that exists; the whole world comes into existence by the power of his creative Word. Consequently, his creation is dear to him, for it was willed by him and "made" by him. The second important element now emerges: this God loves man. The divine power that Aristotle at the height of Greek philosophy sought to grasp through reflection, is indeed for every being an object of desire and of love—and as the object of love this divinity moves the world—but in itself it lacks nothing and does not love: it is solely the object of love. The one God in whom Israel believes, on the other hand, loves with a personal love. His love, moreover, is an elective love: among all the nations he chooses Israel and loves her—but he does so precisely with a view to healing the whole human race. God loves, and his love may certainly be called *eros*, yet it is also totally *agape*.

The Prophets, particularly Hosea and Ezekiel, described God's passion for his people using boldly erotic images. God's relationship with Israel is described using the metaphors of betrothal and marriage; idolatry is thus adultery and prostitution. Here we find a specific reference—as we have seen—to the fertility cults and their abuse of *eros*, but also a description of the relationship of fidelity between Israel and her God. The history of the love relationship between God and Israel consists, at the deepest level, in the fact that he gives her the *Torah*, thereby opening Israel's eyes to man's true nature and showing her the path leading to true humanism. It consists in the fact that man, through a life of fidelity to the one God, comes to experience himself as loved by God, and discovers joy in truth and in righteousness—a joy in God which becomes his essential happiness: "Whom do I have in heaven but you? And there is nothing upon earth that I desire besides you...for me it is good to be near God" (*Ps* 73 [72]:25, 28).

We have seen that God's *eros* for man is also totally *agape*. This is not only because it is bestowed in a completely gratuitous manner, without any previous merit, but also because it is love which forgives. Hosea above all shows us that this *agape* dimension of God's love for man goes far beyond the aspect of gratuity. Israel has committed "adultery" and has broken the covenant; God should judge and repudiate her. It is precisely at this point that God is revealed to be God and not man: "How can I give you up, O Ephraim! How can I hand you over, O Israel!... My heart recoils within me, my compassion grows warm and tender. I will not execute my fierce anger, I will not again destroy Ephraim; for I am God and not man, the Holy One in your midst" (*Hos* 11:8–9). God's passionate love for his people—for humanity—is at the same time a forgiving love. It is so great that it turns God against himself, his love against his justice. Here Christians can see a dim prefigurement of the mystery of the Cross: so great is God's love for man that by becoming man he follows him even into death, and so reconciles justice and love.

Pope Francis

FROM *ADDRESS OF POPE FRANCIS TO THE PARISH PRIESTS OF THE DIOCESE OF ROME*, MARCH 6, 2014

At the beginning of Lent, it does us good to reflect together as priests on mercy. We all need it. Also the faithful, since as pastors we must extend great, great mercy!

The passage from the Gospel of Matthew that we heard makes us turn our gaze to Jesus as he goes about the cities and villages. And this is curious. Where was Jesus most often, where he could most easily be found? On the road. He might have seemed to be homeless, because he was always on the road. Jesus' life was on the road. He especially invites us to grasp the depths of his heart, what he feels for the crowds, for the people he encounters: that interior attitude of "compassion"; seeing the crowds, he felt compassion for them. For he saw the people were "harassed and helpless, like sheep without a shepherd". We have heard these words so many times that perhaps they do not strike us powerfully. But they are powerful! A little like the many people whom you meet today on the streets of your own neighbourhoods.... Then the horizon broadens, and we see that these towns and villages are not only Rome and Italy; they are the world...and those helpless crowds are the peoples of many nations who are suffering through even more difficult situations....

Thus we understand that we are not here to take part in a pleasant retreat at the beginning of Lent, but rather to hear the voice of the Spirit speaking to the whole Church of our time, which is the time of mercy. I am sure of this. It is not only Lent; we are living in a time of mercy, and have been for 30 years or more, up to today.

...

It is up to us, as ministers of the Church, to keep this message alive, above all through preaching and in our actions, in signs and in pastoral choices, such as the decision to restore priority to the Sacrament of Reconciliation and to the works of mercy.

...

Let us ask ourselves what mercy means for a priest, allow me to say for us priests. For us, for all of us! Priests are moved to compassion before the sheep, like Jesus, when he saw the people harassed and helpless, like sheep without a shepherd. Jesus has the "bowels" of God, Isaiah speaks about it very much: he is full of tenderness for the people, especially for those who are excluded, that is, for sinners, for the sick who no one takes care of.... Thus, in the image of the Good Shepherd, the priest is a man of mercy and compassion, close to his people and a servant to all. This is a pastoral criterion I would like to emphasize strongly: closeness. Closeness and service, but closeness, nearness!...Whoever is wounded in life, in whatever way, can find in him attention and a sympathetic ear.... The priest reveals a heart especially in administering the Sacrament of Reconciliation; he reveals it by his whole attitude, by the manner in which he welcomes, listens, counsels and absolves.... But this comes from how he experiences the Sacrament firsthand, from how he allows himself to be embraced by God the Father in Confession and remains in this embrace.... If one experiences this in one's own regard, in his own heart, he can also give it to others in his ministry. And I leave you with the question: How do I confess? Do I allow myself to be embraced? A great priest from Buenos Aires comes to mind, he is younger than I, he is around the age of 72.... Once he came to see me. He is a great confessor: there are always people waiting in line for him there.... The majority of priests confess to him...He is a great confessor. And once he came to see me: "But Father...."; "Tell me"; "I have a small scruple, because I know that I forgive too much!"; "Pray...if you forgive too much...". And we spoke about mercy. At a certain point he said to me: "You know, when I feel this scruple keenly, I go to the chapel, before the Tabernacle, and I say to Him: Excuse me, but it's Your fault, because it is you who has given me the bad example! And I go away at peace....". It is a beautiful prayer of mercy! If one experiences this in his own regard in Confession, in his own heart, he is able to give it to others.

The priest is called to learn this, to have a heart that is moved. Priests who are — allow me to say the word — "aseptic", those "from the laboratory", all clean and tidy, do not help the Church. Today we can think of the Church as a "field hospital". Excuse me but I repeat it, because this is how I see it, how I feel it is: a "field hospital". Wounds need to be treated, so many wounds! So many wounds! There are so many people who are wounded by material problems, by scandals, also in the Church.... People wounded by the world's illusions.... We priests must be there, close to these people. Mercy first means treating the wounds. When someone is wounded, he needs this immediately, not tests such as the level of cholesterol and one's glycemic index.... But there's a wound, treat the wound, and then we can look at the results of the tests. Then specialized treatments can be done, but first we need to treat the open wounds. I think this is what is most important at this time. And there are also hidden wounds, because there are people who distance themselves in order to avoid showing their wounds closer.... The custom comes to mind, in the Mosaic Law, of the lepers in Jesus' time, who were always kept at a distance in order not to to spread the contagion.... There are people who distance themselves through shame, through shame, so as not to let their wounds be seen.... And perhaps they distance themselves with some bitterness against the Church, but deep down inside there is a wound.... They want a caress! And you, dear brothers — I ask you — do you know the wounds of your parishioners? Do you perceive them? Are you close to them? It's the only question....

Mercy means neither generosity nor rigidity.

Let us return to the Sacrament of Reconciliation. It often happens that we priests hear our faithful telling us they have encountered a very "strict" priest in the confessional, or very "generous", i.e., a *rigorist* or a *laxist*. And this is not good. It is normal that there be differences in the style of confessors, but these differences cannot regard the essential, that is, sound moral doctrine and mercy. Neither the laxist nor the rigorist bears witness to Jesus Christ, for neither the one nor the other takes care of the person he encounters. The rigorist washes his hands of them: in fact, he nails the person to the law, understood in a cold and rigid way; and the laxist also washes his hands of them: he is only apparently merciful, but in reality he does not take seriously the problems of that conscience, by minimizing the sin. True mercy *takes the person into one's care*, listens to him attentively, approaches the situation with respect and truth, and accompanies him on the journey of reconciliation. And this is demanding, yes, certainly. The truly merciful priest behaves like the Good Samaritan...but why does he do it? Because his heart is capable of having compassion, it is the heart of Christ!

We are well aware that *neither laxity nor rigorism foster holiness*. Perhaps some rigorists seem holy, holy.... But think of Pelagius and then let's talk...Neither laxity nor rigorism sanctify the priest, and they do not sanctify the faithful! However, mercy accompanies the journey of holiness, it accompanies it and makes it grow.... Too much work for a parish priest? It is true, too much work! And how do we accompany and foster the journey of holiness? Through pastoral suffering, which is a form of mercy. What does pastoral suffering mean? It means suffering for and with the person. And this is not easy! To suffer like a father and mother suffer for their children; I venture to say, also with anxious concern....

FROM *HOMILY*, FEBRUARY 15, 2015

"Lord, if you choose, you can make me clean"... Jesus, moved with compassion, stretched out his hand and touched him, and said: "I do choose. Be made clean!" (*Mk* 1:40–41). The compassion of Jesus! That *com-passion* which made him draw near to every person in pain! Jesus does not hold back; instead, he gets involved in people's pain and their need...for the simple reason that he knows and wants to show *com-passion*, because he has a heart unashamed to have *"compassion"*.

"Jesus could no longer go into a town openly, but stayed in the country; and people came to him from every quarter" (*Mk* 1:45). This means that Jesus not only healed the leper but also took upon himself the marginalization enjoined by the law of Moses (cf. *Lev* 13:1–2, 45–46). Jesus is unafraid to risk sharing in the suffering of others; he pays the price of it in full (cf. *Is* 53:4).

Compassion leads Jesus to concrete action: *he reinstates the marginalized!* These are the three key concepts that the Church proposes in today's liturgy of the word: the *compassion* of Jesus in the face of *marginalization* and his desire to *reinstate*.

Marginalization: Moses, in his legislation regarding lepers, says that they are to be kept alone and apart from the community for the duration of their illness. He declares them: "unclean!" (cf. *Lev* 13:1–2, 45–46).

Imagine how much suffering and shame lepers must have felt: physically, socially, psychologically and spiritually! They are not only victims of disease, but they feel guilty about it, punished for their sins! Theirs is a living death; they are like someone whose father has spit in his face (cf. *Num* 12:14).

In addition, lepers inspire fear, contempt and loathing, and so they are abandoned by their families, shunned by other persons, cast out by society. Indeed, society rejects them and forces them to live apart from the healthy. It excludes them. So much so that if a healthy person approached a leper, he would be punished severely, and often be treated as a leper himself.

True, the purpose of this rule was *"to safeguard the healthy"*, *"to protect the righteous"*, and, in order to guard them from any risk, to eliminate "the peril" by treating the diseased person harshly. As the high priest Caiaphas exclaimed: "It is better to have one man die for the people than to have the whole nation destroyed" (*Jn* 11:50).

Reinstatement: Jesus revolutionizes and upsets that fearful, narrow and prejudiced mentality. He does not abolish the law of Moses, but rather brings it to fulfillment (cf. *Mt* 5:17). He does so by stating, for example, that the law of retaliation is counterproductive, that God is not pleased by a Sabbath observance which demeans or condemns a man. He does so by refusing to condemn the sinful woman, but saves her from the blind zeal of those prepared to stone her ruthlessly in the belief that they were applying the law of Moses. Jesus also revolutionizes consciences in the Sermon on the Mount (cf. *Mt* 5), opening new horizons for humanity and fully revealing God's "logic". The logic of love, based not on fear but on freedom and charity, on healthy zeal and the saving will of God. For "God our Saviour desires everyone to be saved and to come to the knowledge of the truth" (*1 Tim* 2:3–4). "I desire mercy and not sacrifice" (*Mt* 12:7; *Hos* 6:6).

Jesus, the new Moses, wanted to heal the leper. He wanted to touch him and restore him to the community without being "hemmed in" by prejudice, conformity to the prevailing mindset or worry about becoming infected. Jesus responds immediately to the leper's plea, without waiting to study the situation and all its possible consequences! For Jesus, what matters above all is reaching out to save those far off, healing the wounds of the sick, restoring everyone to God's family! And this is scandalous to some people!

Jesus is not afraid of this kind of scandal! He does not think of the closed-minded who are scandalized even by a work of healing, scandalized before any kind of openness, by any action outside of their mental and spiritual boxes, by any caress or sign of tenderness which does not fit into their usual thinking and their ritual purity. He wanted to reinstate the outcast, to save those outside the camp (cf. *Jn* 10).

There are two ways of thinking and of having faith: we can fear to lose the saved and we can want to save the lost. Even today it can happen that we stand at the crossroads of these two ways of thinking. The thinking of the doctors of the law, which would remove the danger by casting out the diseased person, and the thinking of God, who in his mercy embraces and accepts by reinstating him and turning evil into good, condemnation into salvation and exclusion into proclamation.

These two ways of thinking are present throughout the Church's history: *casting off* and *reinstating*. Saint Paul, following the Lord's command to bring the Gospel message to the ends of the earth (cf. *Mt* 28:19), caused scandal and met powerful resistance and great hostility, especially from those who demanded unconditional obedience to the Mosaic law, even on the part of converted pagans. Saint Peter, too, was bitterly criticized by the community when he entered the house of the pagan centurion Cornelius (cf. *Acts* 10).

The Church's way, from the time of the Council of Jerusalem, has always been the way of Jesus, the way of mercy and reinstatement. This does not mean underestimating the dangers of letting wolves into the fold, but welcoming the repentant prodigal son; healing the wounds of sin with courage and determination; rolling up our sleeves and not standing by and watching passively the suffering of the world. The way of the Church is not to condemn anyone for eternity; to pour out the balm of God's mercy on all those who ask for it with a sincere heart. The way of the Church is precisely to leave her four walls behind and to go out in search of those who are distant, those essentially on the "outskirts" of life. It is to adopt fully God's own approach, to follow the Master who said: "Those who are well have no need of the physician, but those who are sick; I have come to call, not the righteous but sinners" (*Lk* 5:31–32).

In healing the leper, Jesus does not harm the healthy. Rather, he frees them from fear. He does not endanger them, but gives them a brother. He does not devalue the law but instead values those for whom God gave the law. Indeed, Jesus frees the healthy from the temptation of the "older brother" (cf. *Lk* 15:11–32), the burden of envy and the grumbling of the labourers who bore "the burden of the day and the heat" (cf. *Mt* 20:1–16).

In a word: *charity cannot be neutral, antiseptic, indifferent, lukewarm or impartial! Charity is infectious, it excites, it risks and it engages! For true charity is always unmerited, unconditional and gratuitous!* (cf. *1 Cor* 13). Charity is creative in finding the right words to speak to all those considered incurable and hence untouchable. Finding the right words.... Contact is the language of genuine communication, the same endearing language which brought healing to the leper. How many healings can we perform if only we learn this language of contact! The leper, once cured, became a messenger of God's love. The Gospel tells us that "he went out and began to proclaim it freely and to spread the word" (cf. *Mk* 1:45).

Dear new Cardinals, this is the "logic", the mind of Jesus, and this is the way of the Church. Not only to welcome and reinstate with evangelical courage all those who knock at our door, but to go out and seek, fearlessly and without prejudice, those who are distant, freely sharing what we ourselves freely received. "Whoever says: 'I abide in [Christ]', ought to walk just as he walked" (*1 Jn* 2:6). Total openness to serving others is our hallmark, it alone is our title of honour!

Consider carefully that, in these days when you have become Cardinals, we have asked Mary, Mother of the Church, who herself experienced marginalization as a result of slander (cf. *Jn* 8:41) and exile (cf. *Mt* 2:13–23), to intercede for us so that we can be God's faithful servants. May she—our Mother—teach us to be unafraid of tenderly welcoming the outcast; not to be afraid of tenderness. How often we fear tenderness! May Mary teach us not to be afraid of tenderness and compassion. May she clothe us in patience as we seek to accompany them on their journey, without seeking the benefits of worldly success. May she show us Jesus and help us to walk in his footsteps.

Dear new Cardinals, my brothers, as we look to Jesus and our Mother, I urge you to serve the Church in such a way that Christians—edified by our witness—will not be tempted to turn to Jesus without turning to the outcast, to become a closed caste with nothing authentically ecclesial about it. I urge you to serve Jesus crucified in every person who is emarginated, for whatever reason; to see the Lord in every excluded person who is hungry, thirsty, naked; to see the Lord present even in those who have lost their faith, or turned away from the practice of their faith, or say that they are atheists; to see the Lord who is imprisoned, sick, unemployed, persecuted; to see the Lord in the leper—whether in body or soul—who encounters discrimination! We will not find the Lord unless we truly accept the marginalized! May we always have before us the image of Saint Francis, who was unafraid to embrace the leper and to accept every kind of outcast. Truly, dear brothers, the Gospel of the marginalized is where our credibility is at stake, is discovered and is revealed!